CW00631176

A NEW
HEALTHY YOU!

Super Juicing

igloobooks

igloobooks

Published in 2017
by Igloo Books Ltd
Cottage Farm
Sywell
NN6 0BJ
www.igloobooks.com

Cover image: (bl) twomeows / © Getty images
Additional cover and interior imagery: © iStock / Getty images

HUN001 1017
2 4 6 8 10 9 7 5 3 1
ISBN 978-1-78810-618-4

Cover designed by Nicholas Gage
Edited by Jasmin Peppiatt

Printed and manufactured in China

Contents

Introduction

'You are what you eat,' or so the saying goes. Never more so has this been true, in an age where it is all too easy to overfill our bodies with processed foods, refined carbohydrates and additives. Yet what if the things we eat are fresh, tasty, appetising and full of goodness? It is possible to make this change to our diets – and juicing is a quick, simple and enjoyable way to do so.

Juice and more

Modern-day juicing is so much more than simply extracting the juice from fruit. Armed with a decent juicer that can handle the tough stuff (such as carrots and pineapple skins), you can create delicious and nutritious concoctions. These tasty drinks can add another dimension to your diet – substitute a healthy juice in place of a naughty snack.

If you cannot forgo the snacks, drink a low-calorie juice, too! Consuming a juice or smoothie is an excellent way to kick-start your day and pack vitamins into your diet.

The recipes in this book will provide you with new juice and smoothie ideas, and are categorised into four useful chapters: **fruit juices, vegetable juices, smoothies** and **mega healthy** drinks.

Why juice?

What's so great about juicing? Why not just eat a few more raw carrots or add some spinach to your evening meal instead of reaching for the 'naughty treats' cupboard?

Five-a-day is the way

Put simply, adding a single juice to your daily food intake can help you reach your five-a-day target of fruit and vegetables more easily. Juices (and smoothies) usually contain only raw ingredients, so fewer minerals and vitamins are lost than during the cooking process.

Juice benefits

Juices can make a difference to what you see on the outside and how you feel on the inside. There are juice recipes to boost immunity, lift your energy levels and help you refuel after exercise. The right juices can lead to clearer skin, stronger teeth and nails, reduced allergies and better sleep.

How it works

Why are vegetables and fruit thought to be of more benefit in their liquid form? Ambassadors of juicing claim that they can boost a sluggish digestive system, allowing your body to absorb many more nutrients than it would if you crunched on an apple or picked your way through a plateful of curly kale.

Less technically, juicing also allows you to consume far larger amounts of healthy vegetables than if you had to sit and eat them. It is also easier to mix it up, introducing a variety of foods that you would not include as part of a meal or to take in foods that do not appeal to you. You can disguise individual tastes when they are blended in a cocktail of fruit-and-vegetable deliciousness.

KEEPING IT IN
Juicing retains more than 90% of the nutrients in fruit and vegetables.

Juicing to lose weight

Small changes to your daily diet can have great health effects – but what if your main goal is weight loss? There are two approaches: the first is to cut out all the foods you know are bad for you (because no matter how we justify it, a slice of carrot cake is an indulgence, not a slimming aid), and replace them instead with vibrant, vital nutrients in juice form. This can be a slow but steady way to drop pounds gradually, over weeks and months. Research shows that it works and you will feel cleansed and energised in the process.

Juicing to cleanse

The second approach involves a more radical attack on body fat. This is the 'juice cleanse'. Advocates of juice cleanses say that if the ingredients are chosen carefully, the right mixture of juices can sustain your body for days at a time, without taking on board any other foods. There are several cleansing programmes available, including DIY plans found in books or online. There are also plans where you order everything for your cleanse and it comes ready to drink.

Each type of plan should provide you with regular juice 'meals' and sufficient calories for your body to function without impairment. You will find that you are having juices every two to three hours to stave off hunger pangs and keep your energy levels topped up. Some programmes recommend sticking to your usual exercise regime, while others suggest you limit yourself to light exercise, such as walking and yoga. Be sensible in your approach: if you are a marathon runner, you will not want to lose your levels of fitness but may have to reduce your daily distance. If you're not an exercise junkie, do not suddenly throw yourself into a new cycle of boxing and bootcamps – listen to your body!

CLEANSE, NOT FAST

A juice cleanse is not a 'fast'. You are not cutting out food, merely choosing to take in calories and nutrients through juice alone. Ensure that you drink 1.6 litres (3 ½ pints) of water each day.

Body basics

Generally speaking, people juice for one of three reasons: to bump up their intake of nutrients, to cleanse or detox their body or to lose weight. How does juicing – rather than simply eating lots of fruit and vegetables – work?

Busting toxins?

Proponents of the juice cleanse – drinking juice, water and nothing else – claim that it will rid your body of toxins and deliver a host of nutrients to your body in their most readily digestible form. Their theory is that the juicing process predigests the food for you, giving your gut a rest and allowing your body to preserve energy that it would normally use during the digestive process.

However, there are those who refute these claims. There are concerns that juicing diminishes the amount of nutrients and fails to provide healthy levels of fibre, protein and the right fats. It is argued that the whole notion of 'detoxing' is redundant, as the body has its own systems in place to do exactly that. They warn also about the dangers of cutting down calories to the point that your metabolism slows, or the weight piles straight back on when you start eating normally again. This book takes into account all of this information, and will guide you on the safest and most effective way to enjoy juices.

Goodness in a glass

What experts all agree on is that juicing, in moderation, can have its benefits. A fresh juice made from organic vegetables is always going to be a healthy alternative to pizza. Drinking freshly-squeezed juice will certainly boost your intake of fruit and vegetables, especially if you are the kind of person who avoids the green bits in meals. Smoothies, which use the whole fruit, are a good compromise as long as they do not increase your calorie intake by too much. Juicing is also a great way to take a look at what you are putting inside your body, and ultimately, to feel like you are controlling your food rather than the other way around.

Home and away

There is much talk these days about the hidden dangers of fruit juices and smoothies. Some research claims that they contain high levels of natural sugars, are lacking in fibre and can cause spikes in blood sugar levels, plus their sweet taste can lead to an addiction to sugary foods and can dull sensitivity to sweetness. So why undertake a new lifestyle that advocates drinking fruit juice?

Taking control of the contents

The answer is simple: your homemade juices will be nothing like the juices you buy at the supermarket or coffee shop. By making your own juices, you are taking control of what is in them. Your recipes will retain more fibre than shop-bought juices. Fibre slows down your digestion (keeping you fuller for longer) and the amount of natural sugars that are absorbed.

Buyer beware!

Treat yourself at a smoothie bar, and you are sometimes likely to be buying a glorified milkshake containing fruit concentrates instead of whole fruit. This lowers the vitamin values of the drinks. They commonly have high sugar levels and a large calorie count. Cartons of juice and smoothies are often pasteurised to extend their shelf-life and contain a whole list of additives. They simply are not the same as the freshly juiced recipes you can make for yourself. Grab a juice on the go from a juice bar, and you will also pay a high price, whether it's healthy or not.

The simple rule is to prepare your own juices at home so you know exactly what you are getting. You have bought the produce, you've chosen what you add, and after reading this book, you will know the benefits you are getting out of it.

KEEP IT QUICK

Juices are best drunk within 20 minutes of making them. After this time, their nutritional value begins to drop.

Fitting it in

The secret to successful, enjoyable juicing is making it work for your lifestyle. There is no denying it: juicing at home (rather than buying pre-prepared juices) can be messy and often takes a lot of preparation and organisation. Taking juices out and about to fit your timetable can be tricky. However, with some careful preparation and planning, it can be done.

Some juices, and most smoothies, can be prepared in advance and taken out with you. You will need a decent flask to keep them cool, and may find you have to stir them if they have separated into a foamy layer with clearer liquid underneath.

Juicing for a day

If you embark upon a whole day juice-fest (that is fest, not fast!), you should find that you are actually in the kitchen for less time than you usually are. It takes around ten minutes to prepare a juice and clean up afterwards. Compare that to the hour that passes trying to put together a nutritiously balanced main course, or 20 minutes spent perusing the shelves until you settle for beans on toast.

Can I still exercise?

Not only can you still exercise, but you must. Any plan that cuts out exercise is an unhealthy one. If you are supplementing your normal diet with juices, then you should find your energy levels are boosted, not reduced. Several ingredients included in the recipes will actually be of benefit when you exercise. The juices are a natural, healthy, isotonic alternative to calorie-laden 'sports drinks', which may be packed with artificial sweeteners, preservatives and other chemicals.

In addition, juices provide much-needed fluids to replace those lost during sporting activity. They contain carbohydrates in a lower-fibre, lower-bulk form that are quickly taken on board. They provide nutrition when you need it the most.

Side effects

If you have chosen to drink nothing but juices for a day or two, you may find your body reacting in unexpected ways. Hunger is a distracting side effect. Headaches are a common complaint, and you may feel more fatigued than you usually do. Stick with it, because these symptoms are your body's way of recalibrating, and you will get through it. If your symptoms do not desist within two days or after returning to solid food, you should see your doctor.

Beating a headache

Headaches commonly occur because you have cut out caffeine and refined sugar. Try not to resort to tablets; after all, you are focusing on a cleaner, healthier body. Instead, get active. The endorphins released when you move your body are natural painkillers, and working out can boost oxygen flow through your body and blood flow to your brain. Ginger is also a natural headache remedy, relaxing the blood vessels and relieving tension, so add some to your juice.

Eat your greens

Many people are surprised to find that, once their bodies are used to juices, they are not actually hungry. However, if you do still find yourself feeling hungry, there are ways and means of beating hunger pangs. Firstly, try to 'chew' your veggie-based juices – it feels more like you are eating normally. If necessary, mimic your everyday eating patterns. Serve your juice in a bowl and eat it like soup. Sit at the table and read, or chat with your family, just as you would with a plate of food in front of you. Try not to grab your juice on the go, but make it into a mealtime like any other food.

KICK-START YOUR SYSTEM

Chewing your juice stimulates your salivary glands, which in turn warn your stomach to expect food pretty soon. The brain sends messages to your digestive system, warning it of the type of food that is on its way.

Getting started

You will be able to make many of the recipes in this book with just a blender but, for others, you will need a good quality juicer. Once you have that, your shopping list will consist mostly of fresh fruit and vegetables; buy organic where possible. If you plan to drink your juices on the move, you will also need a vacuum flask (to keep them fresh) or a leak-proof sports bottle.

Which juicer is best?

There are so many juicers on the market nowadays that it is hard to know which one to buy. If you can afford it, go for at least a mid-price model; you really do get what you pay for. The main choice is between centrifugal or masticating juicers.

Centrifugal juicers use a rapidly spinning sieve basket with a serrated cutting blade at the bottom to separate the juice from the pulp. They are noisy but faster to use, and easier to clean and store than masticating juicers. Try to buy one with a large feeder tube, so you spend less time chopping your ingredients to fit into the machine.

If budget is not a problem, you may want to invest in a masticating juicer. Also known as slow-speed or cold-press juicers, they produce less heat, which reduces the oxidation of the juice – meaning it retains more nutrients. It also means you will be able to store your juice for much longer (sometimes up to 48 hours). However, you will end up spending more time making your juices as the feeder chute is generally smaller. Masticating juicers can be extremely pricey, but often come with extra attachments for making ice cream, extracting pasta, grinding coffee or mincing. Fans of this type of juicer will also tell you that the juices retain more pulp, meaning they have more fibre and even some protein. The thicker consistency allows you to chew on your juice or water it down a little for drinking.

ICE IS NICE

Most fresh juices benefit from being served cold, so stock up on ice; try keeping ice cubes in a paper bag in your freezer to stop them from sticking together.

The garden gang

You may be surprised at how many fruits and vegetables can be juiced. Each has its own benefits. Some boost the nutritional value of a recipe, while others add sweetness to prevent a juice being overly bitter or earthy.

Carrots: every juicer's friend, carrots are bursting with goodness. Juicing carrots benefits your body by making beta-carotene more available and absorbed more efficiently than eating them raw.

Apples: these will form the bulk of many recipes, especially on a juice-cleanse. Apples are a great antioxidant and their sweet, zingy taste compliments other less-palatable ingredients.

Pineapples: another fruit that bulks out your juices; a quarter of a pineapple will add several ounces to your drink. They can be sweet but, if you juice the skins, this will counteract the sweetness. The flesh adds a satisfying thickness if you blend a little into your juice at the end.

Leafy greens: this term is a catch-all for kale, chard, spinach, collard greens, rapini, bok choi, cabbage and romaine lettuce. They contain many vital vitamins and minerals.

Ginger: it is neither fruit nor vegetable but it works really well in juices. It does not need to be peeled, but use it sparingly as it has a very powerful taste. It has so many health benefits, helping to tame nausea, treat colds, fight off infection and it acts as an antiseptic and antihistamine, among many other things.

Beetroot: this root has a powerful effect on the appearance of your juices, and also on your body. It helps your body fight against many complaints. It is something of an acquired taste, variably described as very sweet and delicious or tasting a little like dirt.

IT'S A NO-NO

Banana, avocado, papaya and similar soft fruits don't juice at all well. They do, however, boost your juices, so can be mixed with the juice at the end of the process in a blender or liquidizer. Alternatively, they are great in smoothies.

Supplements

One of the main arguments against the health benefits of juicing is that it cuts out valuable elements of your food, such as fibre and calcium. If you are simply adding a juice shot at the start of the day, or using a smoothie as a tasty snack or post-exercise pick-me-up, then you have no need to worry. If, however, you are using juices as your main food source during a cleanse or detox programme, you should consider supplementing the juices with some other items.

Wheatgrass Fans of juicing constantly sing the praises of this gloriously green stuff. Described as 'liquid sunshine', it gets its vibrant green from the high levels of chlorophyll it contains. Among the many benefits claimed are its powers to fight off colds and fevers and to improve digestion and cleanse the system. It is said to be a powerful antioxidant. It can be juiced on its own and drunk as a shot, or added to other juices in fresh or powdered form. It is worth noting that centrifugal juicers cannot extract juice from fresh wheatgrass.

Psyllium husk This high-fibre ingredient is suggested on week-long juice cleanses to prevent constipation and keep the intestine and bowel functioning properly. It is mixed into the juices. Alternatively, chia seeds can be added to your recipes to increase the fibre levels, and also contribute to your levels of omega-3 fatty acids, protein and antioxidants. Chia seeds are easy to use – generally, soaking them in water for a couple of hours is all you need to get started.

Probiotics Said to have a beneficial effect on the gut, probiotics ('friendly' bacteria, such as acidophilus) supplement the body's own naturally occurring micro-organisms within the digestive system. They can be bought as freeze-dried powders, capsules and tablets and added to your juices and smoothies. Alternatively, you can make your smoothies with bio-live yogurts which contain this 'friendly' bacteria (remember that this will make your smoothies a little thicker than usual).

Spirulina Usually sold as powder or flakes, spirulina comes from blue-green algae, which is nutritionally rich in vitamins and minerals, with some protein and fatty acids. It can be tricky to mix into juices, so use a blender as the final stage of your preparation.

Nuts A great form of protein and fibre, nuts can be juiced in a masticating juicer after soaking overnight in filtered water. Strain off the soaking water and juice with an equal amount of nuts and fresh water. The nut milk is especially delicious when used in smoothies. Try to use fresh, raw (unpasteurised) nuts such as almonds, hazelnuts, walnuts and pecans.

Cut it out

While you are treating your body to the benefits of juices, you should consider what else you are putting into your system. Try to cut out any drinks that you know are counter-effective: the worst culprits are coffee, alcohol and sugary squash or fizzy drinks. You will really ring the changes if you increase the amount of water you drink each day.

Fancy a brew?

There are several drinks you can substitute if you want something other than water. Herbal teas are caffeine-free and offer their own benefits beyond quenching your thirst. If you fancy a fruit tea, check the packet before you boil the kettle. Many fruit teas are blended from synthetic ingredients to give them their fruitiness.

The best approach is to brew your own. Start the day with lemon tea by simply putting a slice of lemon in a cup with hot (not boiling) water. Most citrus fruits make delicious tea, but the vitamin content can be quashed by using boiling water.

Towards the end of the day, try chamomile tea or fennel tea. Fennel has an aniseed taste and many health bonuses: it is a diuretic and has anti-spasmodic properties that will relax the intestinal muscles, making it good for constipation or flatulence. You can make it from fennel seeds (crush and cover with hot water) or use fennel stalks steeped in hot water.

Fresh peppermint tea is a wonderful aid to digestion and also good before bedtime. Experiment with different mint leaves to see if you have a personal preference: apple mint and spearmint both work well but have subtly different tastes.

SACK THE SODAS

Fizzy drinks are the complete antithesis of healthy juices. They are high-calorie concoctions of dyes, preservatives, corn syrup, sweeteners and sometimes BVO (brominated vegetable oil), which is linked to nerve disorders and memory loss (and is used to make some plastics flame retardant).

How to juice

If the only juice you are used to is that from freshly-squeezed oranges, then juicing is going to be something of a shock. One of the beauties of the juices and smoothies is just how flavoursome they are.

Preparation? What preparation?

You can juice most fruits and vegetables without much preparation. Wash them and chop them into chunks to suit the size of your juicer. You can juice unwaxed citrus peel, pineapple skins, apple cores, carrot tops and celery leaves. However, you should not juice or blend fruit stones (peach, nectarine and apricot stones may produce symptoms of cyanide poisoning) and avocado or banana skins.

The biggest hassle is the cleaning and washing up, and getting rid of the pulp and sticky stains. However, get into good juicing habits, as follows:

- Line the pulp collection container with a bag before you begin

- Run a sink full of hot, soapy water

- Prepare your juice, pour it into a glass and put it in the fridge

- Tidy up before you drink: throw out the bag of pulp, wipe down sticky surfaces and wash your juicer

Shop savvy

Where possible, buy organic fruit and vegetables. Choose fruits at the peak of their ripeness for the highest nutritional value. Avoid anything bruised, over-ripe or not ripe enough. Under-ripe fruits are tougher on the digestive system. Where possible, stick to local, in-season produce. This is a better guarantee of quality; out-of-season crops may have been forced to ripeness and over-fertilised.

DON'T BE LAZY
Don't fall into the trap of leaving your dishwasher to do your dirty work. It might leave the jug section of your juicer spotless, but it will not work well on the mesh.

The comedown

You may work your way slowly into a more healthy lifestyle, finding that it's not so hard after all. Alternatively, you may hurtle headlong into your new juicing regime, casting aside all solids.

Whatever your approach, it is important to plan ahead for the days when you reintroduce solid food to your meal times. For example, it is important not to go straight into eating three filling meals per day after having a three-day long juice cleanse.

Beating the cravings

Some people crave specific foods after a juice cleanse. However, your body needs a gentle reintroduction to foods that genuinely, properly need chewing. The chances are, if you rush straight out and devour a three-course meal at a great restaurant, you are going to suffer for it afterwards.

Begin by grazing on small meals consisting mostly of salads and fruit. Soup will continue your diet of easy-to-digest, vitamin-rich, vegetable-based foodstuffs. Do not tackle dairy, meat or starchy carbohydrates too soon and start with brown rice and steamed fish. Keep up the good work by snacking on raw, unsalted nuts and raw vegetables. Try not to go back to your old habits of eating ready meals or giving in to takeaways.

Slowly does it

Eat your food slowly – not just on your first ways back after a juice cleanse, but all the time. Take smaller bites, chew for longer and really savour the food in your mouth. This will help your digestion and your enjoyment of food, and reduce stress levels in today's "do it all, do it fast, do it now" society.

You should also find that you eat less overall; your brain needs 20 minutes to register that you are feeling full, so give it that time before you overeat without even realising.

you can do it

There may be times when you wonder why you have embarked on this crazy way of 'eating'. Be strong and take stock of how you are feeling.

Is it really hunger?

If the overriding sensation is one of hunger, then ask yourself: are you really hungry, or are you just craving foods that you have declared forbidden for the time being? A juice cleanse really does provide all you need to fuel your body but it does not satisfy the need for chocolate, stodge or those oh-so-good-on-your-tongue fats that you would normally allow yourself in moments of weakness.

A healthy choice

You may ask yourself if you have to do this. You have chosen to up your intake of foods that you know are good for you and to decrease the amount of 'bad stuff' you are putting into your body, and you are doing it in a tasty, novel way. Focus on the choices you are making while you pulverise another carrot. Would you sit down and eat four apples and two carrots in one go? Unlikely, and yet with just ten minutes of preparation time, you can have those exact foods in a delicious drink.

Positive thinking

When you start to lose motivation and you find yourself feeling low because of all the things you can't eat, stop and be positive! You have a wide range of foods available to you. You are making new steps to a healthier body that will last for decades. That body allows you to work, exercise and enjoy your friends and family – and all of those things can be done with new levels of energy with the addition of fresh, tasty produce. Let's face it – you've invested in a fairly pricey piece of equipment; it would be a waste to never use it!

A closer look

Your body requires a whole range of nutrients to keep it functioning properly. Choose recipes containing different vegetables and fruit to take in a wide variety of nutrients according to your needs.

Body benefits: minerals

Calcium	Vital for strong bones and teeth, helps to regulate heartbeat, benefits muscle function, nerve transmissions and hormone secretion
Chlorine	Improves liver function, balances fluids in the body, helps produce digestive juices in the stomach
Iodine	Good for healthy skin, nails and hair, assists the thyroid gland, important for energy and growth
Iron	Helps the blood carry oxygen around the body, used for making protein and enzymes, builds muscles
Magnesium	Good for a healthy heart and muscles, needed for bone growth, boosts immunity
Manganese	Helps bones grow and cells function, aids the metabolism of carbohydrates and fats
Phosphorus	Balances body hydration, moves muscles, regulates heartbeat and delivers nutrients to cells, good for strong teeth and bones
Potassium	Maintains heart rhythm and pH balance of blood, used to build proteins, breaks down and uses carbohydrates, good for kidneys, blood pressure, circulation and nerves

Selenium (with vit. E)	Prevents cell damage, enhances liver function, protects against cancer and heart disease, is a powerful antioxidant
Sodium	Balances water in blood and tissue, stimulates muscle and nerve function; too much can lead to high blood pressure
Sulphur	Good for skin, hair, nails and brain and liver function
Zinc	Helps wounds heal, aids hormone and liver function and is an antioxidant

Don't lose it

Your body will try to expel excess sodium (salt). During this process, it binds with calcium, meaning that you will lose a much-needed mineral during the process. That's why we should keep salt (added during/after cooking or hidden in processed foods) to a healthy intake level.

What is an antioxidant?

Antioxidants take various forms and are found in many foods. They help to counteract nasties known as 'free radicals' that are generated in many ways (for example, pollution, smoking, stress, pesticides and drugs). The free radicals have too few electrons and so steal electrons from other molecules, causing damage to the cells in our bodies.

Studies suggest that antioxidant supplements may be of little benefit, but those consumed in foods, such as berries, have a large part to play in keeping us healthy.

Body benefits: vitamins

A (beta-carotene)	The body converts beta-carotene into vitamin A and then uses it to build strong teeth and bones, boost the immune system and protect the digestive and respiratory systems, it is a strong antioxidant.
B1 (thiamine)	Keeps muscles and nerves healthy, helps break down food to release energy.
B2 (riboflavin)	Important for healthy skin, eyes, nails and hair, helps release energy from carbohydrates.
B3 (niacin)	Releases energy from food, good for digestion and the nervous system.
B5 (pantothenic acid)	Helps release energy from food.
B6 (pyridoxine)	Allows the body to store and use energy from carbohydrates and protein, good for skin and blood.
B9 (folic acid)	Used to make red blood cells, repair DNA and avoid tumour growth and genetic disorders.
C (ascorbic acid)	Protects cells, helps wounds heal, needed for healthy tissue, guards against disease and is a powerful antioxidant.
D (calcitriol)	Vital for healthy bones and teeth, this helps your body absorb calcium and phosphorus. Acquired from both food and sunlight.
E (d-alpha-tocopherol)	Protects cells, prevents premature ageing, helps the immune system and circulation and is a powerful antioxidant.
K (phylloquinone)	Needed for blood clotting so helps wounds heal, also good for bone strength.

Food stores

Your body can store fat-soluble vitamins (A, D, E and K), so your daily requirement does
not necessarily need a daily intake. However, water-soluble vitamins (vitamin B-complex and
vitamin C), most often found in fruit and vegetables (and grains) are not stored, so you must
have them more frequently. Any excesses are lost when you urinate. It is vital that you vary
your diet to get the whole range of vitamins and minerals.

Vegetable juices

Vegetable-based juices pack the biggest nutritional punch. Many have fewer calories and sugars than any other drink, depending on the juices and ingredients you choose. Root vegetables can be higher in sugar than other vegetables, but they are still lower in sugar content than many fruits.

Choose your recipes for their vibrant appearance and delicious tastes, but also for their nutritional properties. Carrots and spinach are a fantastic source of beta-carotene, which is good for your eyes and is a great antioxidant.

Many of the following vegetable juice recipes call for some additions of fruit too, to temper the taste, sweeten them and add new textures.

If you want something completely vegetable-rich, choose a drink such as the Carrot and Chilli Juice. Or, if you're happy to have vegetable juices with added fruit, choose something like the Apple, Courgette and Spinach Juice or the Cabbage Juice. There are a whole variety to try and experiment with. Enjoy creating your own vegetable blends too!

SERVES : 1

Preparation time: **10 minutes**

Apple, courgette and spinach juice

50 g / 1 ½ oz spinach
1 courgette (zucchini)
2 green apples

1. Wash the spinach thoroughly to ensure that any grit has been removed.

2. Cut the stem off the courgette and remove some of the skin, as this can be bitter.

3. Pass the ingredients through an electric juicer in the order shown, according to the manufacturer's instructions. The apples may need to be cut into quarters if they are too large to fit.

4. Pour the juice into a glass and serve.

SERVES : 1

Preparation time: **10 minutes**

Green vegetable juice

100 g / 3 ½ oz curly kale

1 lime

1 cucumber

1 green apple

1. Wash the kale and squeeze any remaining moisture from the leaves.

2. Roughly peel the lime, leaving the white pith intact.

3. Pass the ingredients through an electric juicer in the order shown, according to the manufacturer's instructions.

4. Pour into a glass and enjoy.

SERVES : 1

Preparation time: **5 minutes**

Cucumber, tomato and orange juice

2 oranges

½ cucumber

1 tomato

½ lemon, sliced into small segments

a sprig of basil

1. Peel the oranges, keeping as much of the white pith on the fruit as possible.
2. Pass the ingredients (in the order shown) through your electric juicer, according to the manufacturer's instructions.
3. Pour into a glass.
4. Garnish with a slice or two of lemon and a sprig of basil.

SERVES: 1

Preparation time: **10 minutes**

Cabbage juice

¼ head Savoy or other leafy cabbage

75 g / 2 ½ oz spinach

50 g / 1 ²/₃ oz kale leaves

1 celery stick

1 green apple

1. Wash the cabbage, spinach and kale leaves and squeeze out the moisture with your hands.

2. Roughly chop the celery and slice the apple, removing the core as desired.

3. Pass the ingredient in the order shown through an electric juicer, according to the manufacturer's instructions.

4. Pour into a glass for a vegetable juice hit.

SERVES : 1

Preparation time: **10 minutes**

Fresh carrot juice

6-8 carrots (depending on size)

1 lemon

a handful of mint leaves

1. Clean the carrots and cut off the tops.
2. Peel the lemon, keeping the white pith on the fruit where possible.
3. Pass the ingredients through an electric juicer, starting with the mint leaves, according to the manufacturer's instructions.
4. Pour into a glass and garnish with mint, if desired.

SERVES : 1

Preparation time: **10 minutes**

Beetroot juice

175 g / 6 oz beetroot

100 g / 3 ½ oz carrots

1 orange

15 g root ginger

1. Peel the beetroot and wash the carrots, scraping off any grit or dirt.
2. Peel the orange leaving as much of the white pith as possible.
3. Pass the ingredients through an electric juicer, according to the manufacturer's instructions.
4. Pour into a glass and serve.

SERVES : 2

Preparation time: **10 minutes**

Carrot and orange breakfast juice

2 Seville oranges

7 medium carrots

1. Peel the oranges, taking care to leave as much white pith on the fruit as you can, as this contains additional nutrients.

2. Clean and scrub the carrots to remove any dirt.

3. Pass the ingredients through your electric juicer, according to the manufacturer's instructions.

4. Pour into glasses and serve immediately.

5. Sweeten this juice with some organic honey if desired.

SERVES: 2

Preparation time: **5 minutes**

Carrot and apricot juice

8 carrots

3 apricots

1 lemon

2 ½ cm (1 in) piece root ginger

1. Wash and scrub the carrots to remove any dirt.
2. Cut the apricots in half and remove the stone.
3. Peel the lemon leaving the white pith.
4. Pass the ingredients through an electric juicer in the order shown, according to the manufacturer's instructions.
5. Pour into glasses and serve.

SERVES: 1

Preparation time: **5 minutes**

Carrot juice

10 carrots

1 lemon

1. Wash and scrub the carrots to remove any grit or dirt.
2. Peel the lemon, leaving as much white pith on the fruit as possible.
3. Process the ingredients in an electric juicer following the manufacturer's instructions.
4. Pour into a glass and enjoy for a vitamin C hit.

SERVES: 2

Preparation time: **10 minutes**

Spiced tomato juice

1 avocado

a handful of fresh basil and parsley leaves

6 large vine ripened tomatoes

2 celery sticks

a pinch of cayenne

sea salt and freshly ground black pepper

1. Peel and halve the avocado, removing the stone in the process.
2. Using an electric juicer, process the ingredients in the order shown except for the salt and pepper. Use the juicer according to the manufacturer's instructions.
3. Season the collected juice with a pinch of cayenne and the salt and pepper to taste.
4. Pour into glasses and serve.

SERVES : 1

Preparation time: **10 minutes**

kale, lime and red apple

2 red apples

100 g / 3 ½ oz curly leaf kale

1 lime, juiced

a handful of coriander (cilantro)

50 ml / 1 ½ fl. oz / ¼ cup almond milk (optional)

1. Peel and core the apples and chop into chunks.
2. Rinse the kale leaves and squeeze out any excess moisture.
3. Add the chopped apple and kale to the cup of a high-powered blender.
4. Add the lime juice and coriander and blend on a high speed until smooth and combined, according to the manufacturer's instructions.
5. Add the almond milk, if desired, to obtain the consistency you prefer.
6. Pour into a glass and drink for a super green hit.

SERVES : 1

Preparation time: **10 minutes**

Tomato juice

6 medium/large tomatoes

1 green pepper

a handful of parsley

2 celery stalks

½ cucumber

1. Start by chopping the tomatoes and removing the seeds.

2. Cut the pepper in half and remove the seeds and the stalk.

3. Using an electric juicer according to the manufacturer's instructions, pass the ingredients through the juicer in the order shown.

4. Pour into glasses and serve immediately.

5. Alternatively, this can be kept in the refrigerator for up to 48 hours.

SERVES : 1

Preparation time: **10 minutes**

Celery juice

3 celery sticks
1 pear
1 lime
235 ml / 8 fl. oz / 1 cup water

1. Wash the celery to remove any dirt or grit.
2. Core and chop the pear into quarters.
3. Peel the lime leaving the white pith where possible.
4. Pass the ingredients through an electric juicer, according to the manufacturer's instructions.
5. Pour the collected juice into a glass, mix in the water and serve.

SERVES: 1

Preparation time: **15 minutes**

Apple, lemon, ginger and beetroot juice

2 red apples, such as Gala or Braeburn

1 whole beetroot, cooked

2 ½ cm (1 in) piece of root ginger

1 lemon

1. Cut the apples into quarters and remove the core.

2. Peel the beetroot and chop into chunks.

3. Pass the first three ingredients through an electric juicer, according to the manufacturer's instructions.

4. Cut the lemon in half and squeeze the juice into the combined juice and stir.

5. Pour into a glass and serve.

SERVES: 1

Preparation time: **10 minutes**

Carrot, orange and sweetcorn juice

4 carrots

1 orange

50 g / 1 ½ oz / ½ cup sweetcorn, drained

1. Wash and scrub the carrots to remove any grit and dirt.

2. Peel the orange leaving the white pith on the fruit.

3. Pass the ingredients through an electric juicer in the order shown taking care to follow the manufacturer's guidelines.

4. Pour into a glass and serve.

5. Alternatively, this can be kept in the fridge for up to 24 hours.

SERVES: 1

Preparation time: **5 minutes**

Carrot and chilli juice

6 carrots

1 red chilli (chili)

½ red onion

a pinch of black pepper

1. Wash the carrots and scrub to remove any dirt.
2. Halve the chilli lengthways and remove the seeds.
3. Pass the first three ingredients through an electric juicer, according to the manufacturer's instructions.
4. Add the pinch of black pepper to the juice and stir to combine.
5. Pour into a glass for a spicy kick to your morning.

Fruit juices

It is obvious by their taste that some fruits are sweeter than others. Lemons are lower in sugar than oranges, for example. Choose which fruit recipes you are going to try by taking a look at their ingredients and thinking about the health benefits that you require. Having said this, be sure to create a few fruit juices that you wouldn't usually try, as it may surprise you – you may find a new favourite!

If you are trying to cut down on sugars – even those in fruit – lower-sugar fruits include berries such as blueberries, blackberries and raspberries. Citrus fruits are generally lower in sugar content too, such as grapefruit, lemons and limes.

Some fruits, including blackberries and apricots, produce relatively small amounts of juice. Juice recipes may be bulked up by the addition of watery produce such as cucumber and celery.

If you taste your fruit juice and decide that it's still not sweet enough for you, don't be scared to experiment – add a little honey and see if that helps.

From Blueberry Juice or Handmade Orange Juice to Refreshing Orange Soda and Mulberry Cocktail, there are a fantastic variety of fruit juices in this chapter for you to choose from.

SERVES : 1

Preparation time: **10 minutes**

Raspberry lemonade

75 g / 2 ½ oz / ½ cup raspberries

1 tsp pomegranate molasses

1 lime

50 ml / 1 ½ fl. oz / ¼ cup soda water

1. Wash the raspberries and place into a blender with the molasses and blend until smooth.
2. Pass the pulp through a fine sieve and push through with the back of a spoon. Discard any seeds and excess pulp.
3. Juice the lime and add to the raspberry juice.
4. Pour into a glass and top up with the soda water.

SERVES: 2

Preparation time: **10 minutes**

Cherry juice

200 g / 7 oz / 1 ½ cups cherries in light syrup

50 g / 1 ½ oz / ⅓ cup blueberries

1 lemon

1. Pour 150 g of the cherries with the syrup into a blender.

2. Wash the blueberries and add to the cherries and blend on high until smooth, according to the manufacturer's instructions.

3. Pass through a sieve lined with a cheesecloth and collect the juice.

4. Cut the lemon in half and juice, adding to the berry juice.

5. Pour into a glass and add the remaining cherries and lemon wedges as desired.

SERVES : 1

Preparation time: **10 minutes**

Lemon and ginger juice

a thumb-sized piece of root ginger

3 lemons

1 tsp honey

400 ml / 3 ½ fl. oz / 1 ⅔ cup mineral water

a handful of ice cubes

1. Peel the root ginger and place into a blender and whizz to a pulp.

2. Slice the lemons in half and juice then add this juice and the honey to the pulped ginger.

3. Whizz again in the blender, according to the manufacturer's instructions, to mix. Pass through a sieve to remove any large pieces of ginger.

4. Pour into a glass and top up with the water and ice.

SERVES: 1

Preparation time: **5 minutes**

Blueberry juice

1 green apple

100 g / 3 ½ oz / ²/₃ cup blueberries, frozen

½ lime

1. Core the apple and cut into quarters.
2. Pass the apple and blueberries through an electric blender as per the manufacturer's guidelines.
3. Squeeze the lime juice into the collected juice and stir.
4. Pour into a serving glass.

SERVES : 1

Preparation time: **10 minutes**

Sparkling cherry juice

100 g / 3 ½ oz / ²⁄₃ cup ripe red cherries

½ watermelon

100 ml / 3 ½ fl. oz / ½ cup sparkling water

1. Wash and remove the stalks of the cherries before cutting into halves and removing the stones.

2. Cut the watermelon into chunks and discard the skin.

3. Pass the fruit through an electric juicer, according to the manufacturer's instructions.

4. Strain into a glass with ice and top up with sparkling water.

SERVES : 1

Preparation time: **15 minutes**

Pineapple and citrus crush

½ pineapple

2 lemons

1 grapefruit

a handful of ice cubes

a sprig of mint

1. Peel, chop and core the pineapple. Cut into rough 1-inch chunks

2. Using a hand juicer, squeeze the juice from the lemons and grapefruit.

3. Add the pineapple and citrus juice to the cup of a high-powered blender and top up with ice. Blend on high for a minute until combined.

4. Pour into a glass and garnish with a sprig of mint.

SERVES : 1

Preparation time: **5 minutes**

Spiced apple juice

4 apples, such as Gala

1 lemon

½ tsp ground cinnamon

1 tsp organic honey

1. Chop the apples into quarters so that they will fit into your juicer.
2. Peel the lemon leaving as much of the white pith on as possible.
3. Process the apple and lemon through an electric juicer, according to the manufacturer's instructions.
4. Stir in the ground cinnamon and honey to taste.
5. Serve in a glass with ice, if desired.

SERVES : 1

Preparation time: **5 minutes**

Handmade orange juice

4 whole oranges

1. Cut each of the oranges in half and remove the seeds where possible.
2. Squeeze the orange halves over a hand juicer squeezing out as much juice as possible.
3. Scrape some of the pulped orange using a teaspoon and mix with the collected juice.
4. Pour into a glass with some ice.
5. Alternatively, strain into a glass for a smoother juice.

SERVES : 1

Preparation time: **5 minutes**

Cooking time: **20 minutes**

Chilling time: **30 minutes**

Cranberry juice

400 g / 14 oz. / 2 ½ cups fresh
   or frozen cranberries

400 ml / 13 ½ fl. oz / 1 ½ cups water

2 oranges

1 lemon

1 tsp organic honey or light fruit syrup

1. Place the cranberries and water into a saucepan and bring to a boil before reducing to a simmer. Leave for 20 minutes until the berries have popped and broken down.

2. Juice the oranges and lemon using a hand or electric juicer and mix with the honey.

3. Strain the cranberry juice through a fine sieve, reserve the pulp which can be used to flavour cakes or muffins.

4. Mix the strained cranberry juice with the orange, lemon and honey mixture and place in the refrigerator to chill.

5. Serve once chilled or will keep for 48 hours in a sealed container.

SERVES: 1

Preparation time: **10 minutes**

Clementine juice

3 clementines

a handful of ice cubes

1. Cut each of the clementines in half around the centre of the fruit.
2. Using a hand juicer, squeeze as much juice as possible from each of the halves.
3. Scoop out some of the pulp using a spoon and add this to the juice as preferred.
4. Pour into a glass with some ice for a refreshing juice drink.

SERVES : 1

Preparation time: **15 minutes**

Pomegranate juice

2 whole pomegranates
250ml / 9 fl. oz / 1 cup water

1. Cut the pomegranates in half and remove the seeds. This can be done with a pin or by holding them over a bowl and hitting the outer edge with a wooden spoon.

2. Put the seeds into a blender with the water and pulse gently to break the seeds. Do not over blend as this can ruin the juice.

3. Strain the pulp and juice through a fine sieve into a bowl or jug taking care to collect all the juice. You can use a spoon to push the juice through the sieve.

4. Pour into a glass and serve immediately for a healthy morning juice.

SERVES: 2

Preparation time: **10 minutes**

Refreshing orange soda

4 oranges

a handful of ice cubes

500 ml / 1 ¾ fl. oz / 2 cups soda water

1. Peel the oranges, keeping as much of the pith on the fruit as possible.
2. Pass the oranges through your electric juicer, according to the manufacturer's instructions.
3. Fill two tumblers with 4-5 ice cubes each and share the orange juice between them.
4. Top up with the soda water for a healthy and refreshing fizzy drink.

SERVES : 2

Preparation time: **10 minutes**

Spiced orange and apple juice

3 apples

1 orange

2 ½ cm (1 in) piece root ginger

½ lemon

1 tsp ground cinnamon

1. Core and chop the apples into quarters.
2. Peel the orange leaving the white pith.
3. Pass the first three ingredients through an electric juicer, according to the manufacturer's instructions.
4. Juice the lemon half using a manual juicer and mix with the ground cinnamon before stirring into the apple, orange and ginger juice.
5. Pour into glasses with ice.
6. This juice can also be warmed up or topped up with chilled soda water for a longer drink.

SERVES : 1

Preparation time: **10 minutes**

Mulberry cocktail

100 g / 3 ½ oz / ⅔ cup fresh mulberries

1 tsp pomegranate molasses

250 ml / 9 fl. oz / 1 cup water

½ lemon, juiced

a handful of ice cubes

1. Place the berries into a blender and pulse to a pulp.
2. Strain into a bowl through a fine sieve pushing the juice through with a spoon or spatula.
3. Mix with the pomegranate molasses, water and lemon. Pour into a cocktail shaker half-filled with ice and shake.
4. Strain into a glass with ice cubes and top with additional berries if desired.

S E R V E S : 1

Preparation time: **10 minutes**

Mixed orange juice

1 orange

2 clementines

1 blood orange

1 Seville orange

1. Peel all the oranges, leaving the white pith.

2. Pass the fruit through an electric juicer following the manufacturer's instructions.

3. Stir or shake over ice and pour into a glass.

SERVES: 2

Preparation time: **15 minutes**

Coconut, kiwi and pineapple juice

1 coconut

3 kiwi fruits

1 pineapple

1. Carefully break open the coconut, saving the water for later. Spoon out the flesh and set aside.

2. Peel the kiwi fruits and pineapple. Chop into chunks large enough to fit into your juicer.

3. Pass the ingredients through an electric juicer, according to the manufacturer's instructions.

4. Mix the juice collected with the reserved coconut water.

5. Pour into glasses and serve immediately.

SERVES : 1

Preparation time: **5 minutes**

Fresh grapefruit juice

2 grapefruit

1 tsp organic honey

1. Peel the grapefruit leaving as much white pith on the fruit as possible as this contains additional nutrients.

2. Pass the fruit through an electric juicer, according to the manufacturer's instructions.

3. Stir the honey into the juice and taste, adding more honey if desired.

4. Pour into a glass and serve.

SERVES: 2

Preparation time: **10 minutes**

Grape juice

400 g / 14 oz / 2 ½ cups black grapes
100 g / 3 ½ oz / ²/₃ cup blueberries
1 lemon

1. Rinse the grapes and berries in a colander and remove any stems.
2. Place the berries into a blender with a cupful of water. Blend together until you have a thick pulp.
3. Using a fine sieve or muslin cloth, strain the juice from the pulp into a bowl or jug. Discard the pulp.
4. Juice the lemon and add to the grape juice before serving.

SERVES: 2

Preparation time: **10 minutes**

Super orange juice

8 carrots

2 oranges

2 sweet potatoes

2 apples

1. Wash and scrub the carrots to remove any dirt and grit.
2. Peel the orange keeping the white pith intact.
3. Pass the ingredients through an electric juicer, according to the manufacturer's instructions.
4. Shake the collected juice with ice and then pour into serving glasses.

MAKES: 2

Preparation time: **10 minutes**

Fresh pink grapefruit juice

2 grapefruit

3 apples

a handful of ice cubes

sprigs of mint

1. Peel the grapefruit.
2. Pass the 3 apples and 1 grapefruit through an electric juicer, according to the manufacturer's instructions.
3. Chop the second grapefruit into wedges.
4. Half fill two glasses with ice and add the chopped grapefruit. Top with the fruit juice and garnish with sprigs of mint.

SERVES: 2

Preparation time: **10 minutes**

Fresh lemonade

4 lemons

1 tsp honey

a handful of ice cubes

500 ml / 17 ½ fl. oz / 2 cups soda water

1. Using a hand juicer, squeeze the juice from the lemons collecting some of the pulp as you do this.

2. Mix the honey with the lemon juice and place into a blender with a good amount of ice. Blend gently to crush the ice and mix.

3. Pour into glasses and top up with soda water for a refreshing drink.

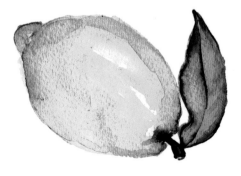

SERVES: 2

Preparation time: **5 minutes**

Refreshing lime and grapefruit juice

2 grapefruit

1 lime

500 ml / 17 ½ fl. oz / 2 cups soda water

1 rosemary sprig

1. Cut the grapefruit into halves and juice using a manual juicer.

2. Roll the lime under your hand on a chopping board to soften it – this will release more juice. Cut into halves and juice with a hand juicer.

3. Combine the two juices in a glass and stir, top up with chilled soda water to make a longer drink.

4. Add ice and a sprig of rosemary.

Smoothies

Smoothies are an effective way to increase your energy levels, particularly before or after exercise, when you don't feel like cooking or eating a large meal. Many smoothie recipes contain some source of calcium, such as milk, and others contain natural sweeteners, such as honey. You will often need a blender to make smoothie recipes and they are best served chilled or over ice, if desired.

Many smoothies are naturally higher in calories than straight juices, so one smoothie per day is a good guideline. Bananas are a fruit with one of the highest sugar contents and differ greatly in size too, so don't overindulge if you are on a serious calorie-controlled diet.

Smoothies can be made out of season using tinned or dried fruits, but watch the calorie count. You can also use frozen fruits such as berries, which will work just as well as fresh fruits.

SERVES: 1

Preparation time: **10 minutes**

Freezing time: **1 hour**

Blueberry smoothie

1 banana

100 g / 3 ½ oz / ²/₃ cup fresh blueberries

100 ml / 3 ½ fl. oz / ½ cup almond milk

1. Peel and chop the banana, place it into a freezer bag and freeze for at least an hour.

2. Wash the blueberries and remove any stalks.

3. Place the ingredients into the cup of a high-powered blender and blend until smooth and well combined.

4. Pour into a serving glass and drink immediately.

SERVES: 1

Preparation time: **10 minutes**

Freezing time: **1 hour**

Tropical smoothie

1 banana

¼ pineapple

100 g / 3 ½ oz / 1 cup mango chunks, frozen

50 g / 1 ½ oz / ½ cup coconut

2 ½ cm (1 in) piece of root ginger

½ red chilli (chili), deseeded

1 lime

1. Peel and chop the banana and place into a freezer bag and freeze for at least an hour.

2. Peel and chop the pineapple.

3. Pass the first five ingredients through an electric blender, according to the manufacturer's instructions.

4. Cut the lime in half and squeeze the juice into the smoothie mixture and stir to combine.

5. Pour into a serving glass and enjoy.

Preparation time: **15 minutes**

Super green smoothie

3 kiwi fruit

75 g / 2 ½ oz / ½ cup raspberries

50 g baby spinach leaves

1 banana

1 lemon

1 tsp chia seeds

1 tsp goji berries

1. Peel and quarter the kiwi fruit and place into a blender with the berries.
2. Wash the spinach leaves and squeeze dry and add to the kiwi and berries.
3. Peel and chop the banana and lemon. Remove the lemon seeds and add to the other fruits.
4. Blend using a high-powered blender, according to the manufacturer's instructions, until thick and combined.
5. Pour into glasses and top with the seeds and goji berries.

SERVES: 2

Preparation time: **20 minutes**

Fresh red berry smoothie

1 banana

75 g / 2 ½ oz fresh strawberries

100 g / 3 ½ oz / ²/₃ cup frozen mixed berries

1. Peel and chop the banana and set aside.

2. Remove the stalk from the strawberries and cut into halves.

3. Add the ingredients to the cup of a high-powered blender and whizz together until thick, according to the manufacturer's instructions. You can add some almond milk or fat-free yogurt if desired.

4. Pour into a glass.

SERVES: 2

Preparation time: **10 minutes**

Strawberry milk smoothie

100 g / 3 ½ oz strawberries
1 banana
500 ml / 17 ½ fl. oz / 2 cups almond milk
a handful of ice cubes

1. Remove the stalks from the strawberries and cut into halves.
2. Peel the banana and roughly chop.
3. Add the fruit to a high-powered blender with the milk and ice cubes. Blend, according to the manufacturer's instructions, on high power until completely smooth and combined.
4. Pour into glasses and serve immediately.

SERVES: 1

Preparation time: **15 minutes**

Freezing time: **1 hour**

Nectarine summer smoothie

1 banana

2 large nectarines

1 large orange

200 ml / 7 fl. oz / 1 cup almond milk

1 tbsp raw honey

1 tsp chia seeds

1. Peel the banana and cut into chunks. Place into a freezer bag and freeze for at least an hour. You can make large batches of frozen banana for regular use.

2. Cut the nectarines into quarters and remove the stone.

3. Peel the orange and separate into quarters removing as many seeds as you can – you do not have to remove all of them.

4. Place all the ingredients, apart from the chia seeds, into the cup of a high-powered blender and blend on high until thick and well combined. Adjust the amount of milk if you prefer a thicker or runnier smoothie.

5. Stir in the chia seeds and pour into a glass and serve.

SERVES: 2

Preparation time: **10 minutes**

Berry and banana drink

1 banana

100 g / 3 ½ oz / ⅔ cup fresh blueberries

50 g / 3 ½ oz / ⅔ cup fresh raspberries

100 ml / 3 ½ fl. oz / ½ cup coconut water

1 lime, juiced

1 handful mixed berries, to serve

2 sprigs of mint, to serve

1. Peel and chop the banana and place into a freezer bag and freeze for at least an hour.

2. Wash the blueberries and remove any stalks.

3. Place the frozen banana, blueberries, coconut water and lime juice into the cup of a high-powered blender and whizz until smooth and well combined.

4. Pour into a serving glass and top with mixed berries and a sprig of mint.

SERVES: 2

Preparation time: **10 minutes**

Black cherry and beetroot smoothie

2 whole beetroots

2 handfuls black cherries

1 red apple

100 ml / 3 ½ fl. oz / ½ cup almond milk

a sprig of mint

1. Peel and roughly chop the beetroot before chopping the cherries in half and removing the stones.

2. Place the beetroot, cherries, apple and almond milk into a high-powered blender and blend on high until combined, according to the manufacturer's instructions.

3. Taste for sweetness and add some organic honey if desired.

4. Pour into a glass and garnish with a sprig of mint before serving.

SERVES : 1

Preparation time: **10 minutes**

Freezing time: **1 hour**

Spinach super seed smoothie

1 banana

1 mango

100 g / 3 ½ oz spinach

1 tsp flax seeds

1 tsp chia seeds

50 g / 1 ½ oz / ¼ cup 0% fat plain yogurt

1. Peel and chop the banana and mango. Place into a freezer bag and place in the freezer for at least an hour.

2. Wash the spinach and squeeze to remove any excess moisture.

3. Place the ingredients into the cup of a high-powered blender and blend until smooth, according to the manufacturer's instructions.

4. Pour into a glass and serve immediately.

5. You can substitute the yogurt for almond milk or similar if you feel it is too thick.

SERVES : 1

Preparation time: **10 minutes**

Freezing time: **1 hour**

Thick orange smoothie

1 mango

2 oranges

1 tsp organic honey

50 ml / 1 ½ fl. oz / ¼ cup almond milk

1. Peel the mango and chop into chunks removing the stone as you go. Place into a freezer bag and freeze for at least one hour.

2. Cut the oranges in half and juice using a hand juicer.

3. Place all the ingredients into the cup of a blender and blend until smooth, according to the manufacturer's instructions.

4. Pour into a glass and serve.

SERVES : 1

Preparation time: **10 minutes**

Kiwi, apple, cucumber and parsley

2 green apples

4 kiwi fruit, peeled

1 bunch parsley

1 cucumber

1 lime

1. Chop the apples into quarters and remove the core.

2. Put the apple quarters, kiwi fruit, cucumber and lime juice in a blender and whizz for 20 seconds or until smooth.

3. Pour into a glass and garnish with some parsley leaves.

SERVES : 1

Preparation time: **10 minutes**

Beetroot and chard smoothie

100 g / 3 ½ oz chard

100 g / 3 ½ oz little gem lettuce

175 g / 6 oz beetroot

2 celery sticks

a handful of ice cubes

1. Wash the chard and lettuce leaves and squeeze out any remaining moisture.
2. Peel and chop the beetroot, and slice the celery into smaller chunks.
3. Fill a third of the cup from a blender with ice cubes and then add the other ingredients. Whizz in a high-powered blender until all ingredients are chopped and well combined.
4. Strain into a glass and enjoy.

SERVES : 1

Preparation time: **10 minutes**

Green fruit smoothie

2 green apples

75 g / 2 ½ oz baby leaf spinach

50 g / 1 ½ oz kale

1 lime

a handful of parsley

1. Chop and core the apples and set aside.

2. Wash the spinach and kale leaves to remove any grit and squeeze to remove remaining moisture.

3. Put the cored apples, spinach, kale, lime juice and a handful of parsley in a blender and whizz until smooth.

4. Pour the smoothie into a serving glass.

SERVES : 1

Preparation time: **15 minutes**

Watermelon smoothie

½ watermelon

1 apple, such as Gala or Pink Lady

100 g / 3 ½ oz / ²⁄₃ cup raspberries

a sprig of mint

1. Cut the watermelon into cubes and discard the skin.

2. Cut the apple into chunks and remove the core.

3. Put the watermelon, apple and raspberries in a blender and whizz, according to the manufacturer's instructions, for around 20 seconds or until smooth and combined.

4. Pour into a glass and top with a spring of mint.

Preparation time: **5 minutes**

Carrot and pear smoothie

2 carrots

2 pears

1 lemon, juiced

1 tsp lavender leaves

1 tsp cayenne pepper, ground

1. Wash the carrots and pears to remove any dirt or grit.

2. Cut the pear into quarters and remove the core.

3. Place the ingredients into a high-powered blender, chop into smaller pieces if necessary, and blend to a thick smoothie.

4. Pour into glasses for a healthy breakfast kick.

SERVES: 1

Preparation time: **10 minutes**

Beetroot and mint smoothie

2 whole beetroots

1 celery stick

1 red apple

a handful of mint leaves

1 tsp cayenne pepper, ground

a sprig of mint

1. Peel and roughly chop the beetroot before chopping the celery and apple.

2. Place the ingredients into a high-powered blender and blend on high until combined, according to the manufacturer's instructions.

3. Taste for sweetness and add some organic honey if a sweeter taste is desired.

4. Pour into a glass and garnish with a sprig of mint.

Mega healthy

This chapter contains both juices and smoothies that are mega healthy due to the ingredients used – many of which are 'superfoods'. They take a variety of ingredients and blitz them together for their varying nutritional qualities, from the useful minerals to vitamins and proteins that they can provide your body.

Some ingredients are included in minimal amounts but really make a difference to both the taste of the drink and the nutrition it provides. Ginger is a great example of this – a small amount makes a big impact on the taste of the drink and the root has an extremely long list of benefits.

Other 'mega healthy' ingredients included in the recipes in this chapter are avocados, chia seeds, celery, kale, parsley, spinach, beetroot, basil and flaxseeds. You can even add these to your favourite juices or smoothies from other chapters – enjoy experimenting!

SERVES : 1

Preparation time: **10 minutes**

Green smoothie

50 g / 1 ½ oz baby leaf spinach

50 g / 1 ½ oz kale

10 g mint leaves

½ pineapple

50 ml / 1 ½ fl. oz / ¼ cup coconut water

1 lime

1. Wash the spinach, kale and mint to remove any grit. Squeeze out any excess moisture.

2. Peel the pineapple and remove the core if tough. Chop into chunks.

3. Place the leaves and pineapple into a high-powered blender and blend until smooth, according to the manufacturer's instructions.

4. Add the coconut water and squeeze in the lime juice and blend again to mix.

5. Pour into a glass and serve.

SERVES: 1

Preparation time: **5 minutes**

Orange and banana smoothie

1 banana

2 oranges

1 tsp organic honey

2 tsp flaxseeds

50 ml / 1 ½ fl. oz / ¼ cup almond milk

1. Peel the banana and slice.
2. Peel the orange and cut into quarters removing the pips as you go.
3. Place all the ingredients into the cup of a blender and whizz for around 20 seconds or until smooth, according to the manufacturer's instructions.
4. Pour into a glass and serve.

SERVES : 1

Preparation time: **10 minutes**

Vegetable and herb smoothie

1 carrot

1 parsnip

½ leek

½ beetroot

50 g / 1 ½ oz baby leaf spinach

10 g fresh basil

10 g flat leaf parsley

1 celery stick

1. Wash the carrot, parsnip and leek to remove any dirt or grit.
2. Pass the first four ingredients through an electric juicer, according to the manufacturer's instructions.
3. Wash the spinach, basil and parsley and squeeze out any excess moisture. Roll together and pass through the juicer followed by the celery stick.
4. Stir the collected juice to combine the ingredients and pour into a serving glass.

SERVES: 1

Preparation time: **10 minutes**

Freezing time: **1 hour**

Avocado and banana smoothie

1 banana

1 avocado

20 g coriander (cilantro)

100 ml / 3 ½ fl. oz / ½ cup coconut water

1 lime, juiced

1. Peel the banana and slice. Place into a freezer bag and freeze for at least one hour.

2. Halve the avocado and remove the stone. Scoop out the flesh and discard the skin.

3. Wash and lightly chop the coriander.

4. Place the ingredients into the cup of a high-powered blender and whizz for around 20 seconds or until smooth, according to the manufacturer's instructions.

5. Pour into a glass and serve immediately.

SERVES : 1

Preparation time: **10 minutes**

Citrus juice

1 grapefruit

1 pink grapefruit

1 orange

1 lime

1 lemon

1. Peel the fruit leaving as much white pith as possible, as this contains additional nutrients.

2. Cut the larger fruits into segments to fit into your juicer.

3. Process the fruit through an electric juicer in the order shown, according to the manufacturer's instructions.

4. Pour the finished juice into a glass and enjoy.

SERVES : 1

Preparation time: **4 hours**

Raspberry and chia lemonade

3 tbsp chia seeds

1 cup water

100 g / 3 ½ oz / ²/₃ cup raspberries

2 lemons, juiced

1 tbsp pomegranate molasses

1. In a bowl, combine the chia seeds with the water and set aside for at least 4 hours so that they create a gel.

2. Using a blender, create a puree of the raspberries by blending for a couple minutes, according to the manufacturer's instructions. Strain this into the chia seed gel and mix in the lemon juice and pomegranate. Add some more water to loosen, if needed.

3. Taste to check sweetness and add more pomegranate if desired.

4. Pour into glasses and drink as it is or top up with sparking water for a longer drink.

SERVES : 1

Preparation time: **5 minutes**

Beetroot juice

1 red apple

1 whole beetroot

3 carrots

1 celery stick

a handful of parsley

½ lemon, juiced

1. Cut the apple into quarters and core. Peel the beetroot to remove the tough outer skin.
2. Wash the carrots and celery to remove any dirt or grit.
3. Pass the first five ingredients through an electric juicer, according to the manufacturer's instructions, starting with the parsley.
4. Add the lemon juice to the rest of the juice and stir together.
5. Pour into a glass and drink immediately.

SERVES : 1

Preparation time: **5 minutes**

Green apple and vegetable juice

4 green apples, such as Granny Smith

2 celery stalks

50 g / 1 ⅔ oz cavolo nero

2 limes

a handful of fresh coriander (cilantro)

2 ½ cm (1 in) piece root ginger

1. Quarter and core the apples.
2. Wash the celery and cavolo nero to remove any grit.
3. Peel the limes as much as possible – too much peel can make the juice bitter.
4. Pass the ingredients through an electric juicer following the list from the bottom up and according to the manufacturer's instructions.
5. Pour into a glass and garnish with additional lime wedges.

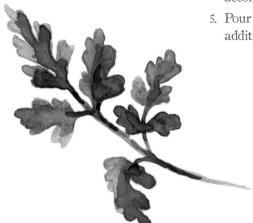

SERVES: 1

Preparation time: **5 minutes**

Raw beetroot juice

1 beetroot

75 g / 2 ½ oz beetroot greens

1 apple, such as Pink Lady

4 carrots

1. Peel the beetroot then roughly chop it.
2. Wash the greens and squeeze out any moisture.
3. Pass the ingredients through an electric juicer in the order shown, according to the manufacturer's instructions.
4. Pour into a glass and drink immediately.

SERVES: 2

Preparation time: **5 minutes**

Cooking time: **30 minutes**

Chilling time: **1 hour**

Honey, lemon and ginger juice

4 lemons

1 large piece root ginger

1 tbsp organic honey

500 ml / 17 ½ fl. oz / 2 cups water

1. Cut the lemons in half and juice using a hand juicer. Place the lemon juice and halves into a saucepan.

2. Roughly chop the ginger and add to the pan with the remaining ingredients.

3. Bring to the boil then turn off the heat and cover. Leave for 30 minutes to steep and for the flavours to infuse.

4. Strain into a sealable jar and place in the fridge to chill for at least an hour. Alternatively, you can drink this hot.

5. Once chilled, pour into glasses and garnish with lemon slices.

SERVES : 1

Preparation time: **10 minutes**

Fresh green juice

2 medium apples

1 green pepper

2 celery sticks

100 g / 3 ½ oz / ²/₃ cup kale

1 cucumber

a handful of parsley

1 lime

1. Core the apples and halve.

2. Cut the pepper in half and remove the seeds and thick stalk.

3. Using an electric juicer, process the ingredients in the order shown, according to the manufacturer's instructions. You can peel the lime first, if desired, as the peel can often be bitter.

4. Stir or shake the juice and pour into a serving glass.

SERVES : 1

Preparation time: **5 minutes**

Spicy carrot juice

12 carrots

1 tsp turmeric

1 tsp cayenne, ground

1 clove of garlic

2 ½ cm (1 in) piece of root ginger

1. Wash the carrots to remove any dirt.
2. Pass the ingredients through an electric juicer, according to the manufacturer's instructions.
3. Stir the collected juice to combine.
4. Pour into a glass and serve.

SERVES : 1

Preparation time: **10 minutes**

Matcha iced tea

½ tsp matcha green tea powder

50 ml / 1 ½ fl. oz / ¼ cup water, plus more
   to top up

1 lime

1 tsp raw honey

1. Place the matcha tea into a bowl with the
   water and whisk thoroughly until there are
   no clumps.

2. Cut the lime into halves and juice using a
   manual juicer.

3. Pour the lime juice and dissolved matcha into
   a glass half filled with ice.

4. Stir in the honey to sweeten.

5. Top up with still or sparking water.
   Alternatively, you could use almond milk.

SERVES: 1

Preparation time: **10 minutes**

Detox beetroot smoothie

1 beetroot

2 apples, such as Gala

4 carrots

1 lemon

1. Peel the beetroot and chop into large chunks.
2. Core the apple and cut into quarters.
3. Wash the carrots and roughly scrape before chopping into chunks.
4. Using a high-powered blender, blend the first three ingredients together until thick and smooth, according to the manufacturer's instructions.
5. Cut the lemon in half and juice. Add this to the other smoothie ingredients and blend again briefly to mix.
6. Pour into a glass and serve immediately.
7. Add some water if it is too thick. The smoothie can also be sweetened with honey or fruit syrup.

Dear diary

So, what's it to be? Are you going to augment your diet with a selection of delicious shots and smoothies, or are you ready for a full-on juice cleanse?

Either way, you should chart your progress so that you have a record of the changes in the way you feel and look. The following pages are split to suit either approach. If you are trying new recipes on a daily basis, use the 'Juice plans and diary' log to note your stats, exercise taken and how the juices fit into your day. If you are cutting out all solids, use the 'My Juice Cleanse' log to note down how you are feeling – physically and mentally – and what results you achieve. It will help to tailor the juicing days to your own requirements so that you are well armed for the next cleanse you undertake.

Juice plans and diary

week 1

	Body stats
Weight:	
Chest measurement:	
Waist:	
Hips:	
Thigh:	
Upper arm:	
Body fat % (if known):	

Juices tried this week				
Page:		When:		Rating:
Page:		When:		Rating:
Page:		When:		Rating:
Page:		When:		Rating:
Page:		When:		Rating:
Page:		When:		Rating:
Page:		When:		Rating:

Exercise log

Juice plans and diary

Week 2

	Body stats
Weight:	
Chest measurement:	
Waist:	
Hips:	
Thigh:	
Upper arm:	
Body fat % (if known):	

Juices tried this week					
Page:		When:		Rating:	
Page:		When:		Rating:	
Page:		When:		Rating:	
Page:		When:		Rating:	
Page:		When:		Rating:	
Page:		When:		Rating:	
Page:		When:		Rating:	

Exercise log

Juice plans and diary

Week 3

	Body stats
Weight:	
Chest measurement:	
Waist:	
Hips:	
Thigh:	
Upper arm:	
Body fat % (if known):	

Juices tried this week

Page:	When:	Rating:
Page:	When:	Rating:
Page:	When:	Rating:
Page:	When:	Rating:
Page:	When:	Rating:
Page:	When:	Rating:
Page:	When:	Rating:

Exercise log

My juice cleanse

Target number of juice-only days:		

	Pre-juice	Post-juice
Weight:		
Chest measurement:		
Waist:		
Hips:		
Thigh:		
Upper arm:		
Body fat % (if known):		

Before

How do you feel?

What do you hope to achieve by juicing?

What preparation have you done?

During

How do you feel?

What is proving hardest?

What are you enjoying?

Exercise log

After

How do you feel?

What has improved the most?

What habits will you continue?

Juices you liked

My juice cleanse

Target number of juice-only days:		

	Pre-juice	Post-juice
Weight:		
Chest measurement:		
Waist:		
Hips:		
Thigh:		
Upper arm:		
Body fat % (if known):		

Before

How do you feel?

What do you hope to achieve by juicing?

What preparation have you done?

After

How do you feel?

What has improved the most?

What habits will you continue?

During

How do you feel?

What is proving hardest?

What are you enjoying?

Exercise log

Juices you liked

Take it away

So, how do you feel? Hopefully you are now full of the joys of spring greens and can really appreciate the benefits brought by adding more fruit and vegetables to your life, and in such a quick, easy way.

Don't forget that a juice cleanse will take its toll on your appetite and on your body's ability to handle solid foods. Heed the warnings and do not dive straight back into a plateful of fish and chips or a full Chinese banquet – your digestive system will not cope.

Instead, ease your way back into eating with delicious salad-based meals, homemade soups and your chosen recipes from this book. Get your teeth into fresh, organic fruits straight from the bowl – no juicing required. Treat yourself to the very best ingredients and you should find that your taste buds crave distinctive tastes, not artificial ingredients – because now they know the difference.

Change the way you think about convenience food. A takeaway is not a reward; it is a step back to your old pre-juicing way of life. It is actually much quicker to fire up your juicer and give your body a proper present, gift-wrapped in a glass. Try to make juicing a daily habit, working your way through the recipes in this book according to your whims at the time. A glowing exterior and healthier insides will be the reward you truly deserve.

Diet consultant: Jo Stimpson

Picture Credits

24 iLight foto/Shutterstock

25t Valentyn75/Dreamstime

127b Yvdavyd/Dreamstime

All other imagery: © iStock / Getty